C901542744

LIBRARIES NI
WITHDRAWN FROM STOCK

KU-165-834

POLAND

UNPACKED

Clive Gifford

WAYLAND
www.waylandbooks.co.uk

First published in Great Britain in 2015 by Wayland
Copyright © Wayland, 2015

All rights reserved

Editor: Nicola Edwards
Designer: Peter Clayman
Cover design: Matthew Kelly

Dewey number: 943.8'0574-dc23
iSBN: 978 0 7502 9157 6
Library eBook iSBN: 978 0 7502 9158 3

Wayland, an imprint of
Hachette Children's Group
Part of Hodder and Stoughton
Carmelite House
50 Victoria Embankment
London EC4Y 0DZ

An Hachette UK Company
www.hachette.co.uk
www.hachettechildrens.co.uk

Printed and bound in China

10 9 8 7 6 5 4 3 2 1

Picture acknowledgements: All images and graphic elements courtesy of
Shutterstock except: p5 (br) and p29 (t) Wikimedia Commons; p14 (b) Alamy.

Every attempt has been made to clear copyright. Should there be any inadvertent
omission, please apply to the publisher for rectification.

The website addresses (URLs) included in this book were valid at the time of
going to press. However, it is possible that contents or addresses may have
changed since the publication of this book. No responsibility for any such
changes can be accepted by either the author or the Publisher.

Contents

Poland: Unpacked

Welcome to Poland! You've travelled to one of Europe's most historic and interesting nations. Geographically, Poland has everything from sandy deserts to snow-topped hills and mountains, large forests and hundreds of lakes. It also boasts a rich culture and history as its people have been at the forefront of science and the arts. So, if you want to learn about crooked houses and equally crooked forests, how duck's blood is used in a popular soup and where you can find Europe's heaviest wild animal, you've come to the right place!

Fact file

Area: 312,679 km²

Population: 38.3 million (July 2014)

Capital city: Warsaw

Main language: Polish

Land borders: Czech Republic, Belarus, Germany, Ukraine, Slovakia, Russia, Lithuania

Currency: The złoty

Poland

You can see on this map how Poland shares land borders with seven other countries. Poland's capital city, Warsaw, is shown too, along with some of the other places you will discover in this book.

Baltic Sea

Lithuania

Russia

Sopot
Gdańsk

Vistula

Narev

Germany

Varta

Poznań

Warsaw

Poland

Łódź

Belarus

Wroclaw

Odra

Lublin

Bledow Desert

Vistula

Kraków

Czech
Republic

Rysy
(highest point)

Ukraine

Tatra Mountains

Slovakia

Krakow
Every hour in Kraków, a trumpeter starts to play then stops. This commemorates the occasion in the 15th century when a trumpeter played to warn the city of an invasion by an army of Tartars, only stopping when he was shot by an invader's arrow.

Szymbark
This upside-down house has been a tourist attraction in the small village of Szymbark since 2007. It took five times longer to build than a regular home. Visitors enter through a 'rooftop' window and inside is a museum to look round.

Wondrous Warsaw

F ew countries have had as many capital cities as Poland, including Płock, Gnierzno, Kraków, Poznań, Łódź and Lublin. Warsaw, though, is the current capital and is the largest in Poland with 1.73 million people living in the city and a further million in the metropolitan area surrounding it.

NO WAY!

The city's symbol, found on shields and many walls in the city is Syrekna – a fighting mermaid armed with a sword. It was already used in the 14th century, when the mermaid was shown with the scales of a dragon.

Castle Square contains the Royal Castle, home of Polish kings in the 16th-18th centuries.

Defying Destruction

Warsaw's motto is *Contemnit procellas* which means, 'It defies the storms'. Warsaw's Old Town district was first built in the 13th century, but has had to be rebuilt a number of times due to its destruction by invading forces. A statue of Sigismund III, who made Warsaw the capital of Poland in 1611, stands in the Old Town's Castle Square. A giant bronze church bell, made in 1646, can also be found in the Old Town. According to local legend, walking round it three times in a row will bring you good luck.

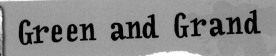

Green and Grand

Warsaw was largely rebuilt after World War II and boasts many parks and grassy areas. In fact, around a quarter of the entire city is green space. The city is located on the banks of the Vistula River and a popular walk inland from the river, known as the Royal Route, takes people past grand parks, avenues and palaces once inhabited by the country's kings and nobles as well as the national parliament and the home of the country's president, Namiestnikowski Palace.

Visitors and locals stroll along Warsaw's Royal Route at night.

Hipster Hangouts

The Palace of Culture and Science towers over the rest of Warsaw.

Warsaw is an exciting city to visit and has plenty of fashionable streets and regions where you can browse the shops, eat and hang out. These include Plac Zbawiciela, Powiśle, Śródmieście and a funky concert space and café housed in the ground floor of Warsaw's tallest building, the grandly-named Palace of Culture and Science. Standing 230.6m high and with its four clock faces added in 2000, it is the tallest clock tower in Europe.

The Land

Poland is the ninth largest country in Europe, a little bigger than Italy or the United Kingdom. It is mostly made up of large, rolling plains, many of which are farmed or used by grazing animals. Don't make the mistake of thinking that Poland's landscapes aren't interesting; the country has some amazing and spectacular features, many of which are contained inside its 23 national parks.

NO WAY!

White storks are found in many parts of the world from China to Morocco, but around a quarter of all storks, over 60,000, live in Poland!

Wood You Believe It?

Poland remains heavily forested. Almost a third of its land is still covered in large areas of trees, a little over half of which are coniferous, including various species of pines. Forests provide homes for animals such as wolves, elk, beavers and wild boars. In one particular forest, the world-famous Bialowłeża Primeval Forest, Europe's heaviest wild animal, the European Bison, lives in small numbers – there are thought to be about 800 of them.

A male European Bison can grow to a weight of 1,000kg.

Mountains and Deserts

Poland's highest point, called Rysy, stands at 2,499m above sea level. It's deep in the Tatra Mountains that form a natural border between parts of Poland and its neighbour, Slovakia. Despite lying in northern Europe, Poland also contains a sandy desert. The Błędów Desert (right) is a real oddity, a 12 km² area of sand 70m deep in some places. The inland mini desert is surrounded by lush plant life.

Water Features

The Vistula River winds its way through the centre of Kraków.

Poland's longest river is the Vistula (also known as Wisla) which snakes its way 1,047km through the country before emptying into the Baltic Sea. The Vistula is connected to other Polish rivers, such as the Oder, through tributaries and canals to provide major waterways. Poland has a staggering 9,300 lakes, over 2,000 of which are found in the Masurian Lakes region in the north-east of the country.

Super Scientists

Poland's scientists have won more than a dozen Nobel Prizes and have made major contributions in many fields – including Henryk Magunski who developed some of the first walkie-talkie radios, Tadeusz Krwawicz who created tools to remove eye cataracts and Leo Gerstenzang who invented the cotton bud! Read on to discover some of the most notable Polish scientists of all.

NO WAY!

The first bulletproof vest was invented by Polish priest, Kazimierz Żegleń. He tested it himself, putting it on and asking a friend to fire a revolver at him. Fortunately, it worked ...phew!

Marvellous Marie

Born in Warsaw, Maria Skłodowska and her husband Pierre Curie discovered two new chemical elements in 1898 – radium and polonium, the latter named after her homeland. Her research into radioactivity was vital for the use of x-rays in medicine, and during World War I she helped equip ambulances with x-ray equipment and even drove them into war zones. Marie Curie became the first woman to teach at France's prestigious Sorbonne Institute and the first to win two Nobel Prizes, for physics in 1903 and chemistry in 1911.

This statue of Marie Curie is in Warsaw, the city of her birth.

Curious Chemists

Polish chemists have made some major breakthroughs. Gdańsk-born Daniel Fahrenheit devised the first mercury-in-glass thermometer in 1714 and also the temperature scale that bears his name. Another Polish chemist, Casimir Funk, discovered the importance of vital amines on the body (his term became shortened to vitamins). He was also the first to isolate a vitamin – B3, also known as niacin.

A new generation of Polish scientists studies at Warsaw's AGH institute of Science and Technology.

Amazing Astronomers

Almost everyone thought the Sun, stars and planets orbited a non-moving Earth until Nicolaus Copernicus observed the night sky and proved the theory wrong. In his landmark book of 1543, he showed how the Earth spins on its own axis, producing an Earth day, and moves through space in orbit around the Sun. It caused a revolution in scientific thinking.

A century later, Johannes Hevelius, mayor of Danzig (Gdańsk), built his own observatory called the Star Castle as well as a giant 46m-long telescope which wobbled in the slightest breeze. Hevelius was no fool though; he discovered four comets and was the first to map the surface of Earth's Moon in detail.

This bronze statue shows Copernicus holding a scientific instrument called an armillary sphere.

Food for Thought

P oland's cuisine features many familiar ingredients, from potatoes, rice and chicken to mushrooms, beef, and cheese, only they're combined or served in slightly unfamiliar ways. A cold beetroot and yoghurt soup called *chłodnik*, for example, is popular in summer, while pizzas in Poland tend to be served with no tomato sauce on the pizza base. Instead, the pizza is served with a large jug of sauce to be poured on top of it.

Get Stuffed!

Poland produces lots of wheat and other cereal crops, so it is no surprise that many Poles eat a lot of different breads. Flour is also used to make other popular foods, such as large pretzels, dumplings and *pierogi*, pockets of dough which are slit and stuffed with fillings such as spiced meats or cheese. Other popular filled foods include stuffed cabbage leaves called *gołąbki*, stuffed peppers and cake rolls with poppy-seed-flavoured fillings.

Some pierogis are filled with fruit and sugar and served with sour cream.

Stuffed cabbage leaves

Oddities on Offer

There are some odd dishes on offer around the country, including *żurek*, a sour rye soup complete with floating sausages, *zupa ogórkowa*, a hot soup made of cucumbers and *smalec*, which is fried pieces of lard! If those dishes don't tickle your tastebuds, there's always *czernina* to consider. It's a soup made of vinegar, sugar, chicken stock and duck blood! Alternatively, there's *flaki*, another popular hot soup made of cow stomach (tripe).

Zupa ogórkowa – cucumber soup

NO WAY!

Wrocław's Piwnica Swidnicka restaurant is believed to have been open for business since 1275, making it one of the oldest restaurants in the world.

Bigging up Bigos

A hearty bowl of bigos

Poland's national dish is called *bigos* and is a type of slow-cooked stew. According to legend, it was introduced to the country by a Lithuanian noble who became King Władysław Jagiełło of Poland in 1385. The stew's ingredients can vary but usually include sauerkraut (fermented cabbage), tomatoes, mushrooms, cuts of meat such as pork, beef, veal and rabbit as well as peppers, juniper berries and prunes. It is often served with rye bread or mashed potato and is warm and filling.

Work and School

Poland used to be all about farming, but today only around one in eight of the country's workers are employed in agriculture. Wheat, barley, rye, potatoes and other vegetables are the leading crops. Service industries such as transport, banking and shops provide jobs for almost two thirds of the workforce, while manufacturing industry holds an important place in the Polish economy.

Off to School

A Polish primary school class.

Schools are free in Poland and education usually runs between the ages of age six and eighteen, with some students leaving school to take apprenticeships at 16. Students study a wide range of subjects, from getting to grips with the Polish alphabet (which contains 32 letters) to learning foreign languages of which English is the most commonly studied, followed by German and French.

Poland was the first country to have a dedicated government ministry of education (in 1773) and its first university was one of the earliest in Europe. The Jagiellonian University was founded in Kraków by King Casimir III in 1364.

Jagiellonian University students number over 50,000 each year.

Mining and Manufacturing

Poland has large coal deposits in the south-west of the country and sulphur, copper, zinc and other metals are also extracted. These help provide materials for large metalworking and chemical industries in Poland. The country is one of Europe's largest manufacturers of buses and over a third of all TVs sold in Europe are from Poland. Increasing numbers of foreign companies have invested in Poland, from Amazon and Toyota to Google and IKEA, whose mega factory in Zbąszynek produces two million tables, chairs and sofas a year.

Chemicals are one of Wloclawek's major industries.

NO WAY!

A common superstition among students is to wear red underwear and to blow on their fingers for luck before the start of an exam.

Working Abroad

Unemployment is often relatively high in some parts of Poland and even when jobs are available, many skilled workers find that they can earn more working abroad in countries such as Germany and the UK. Since Poland joined the European Union in 2004, around one in seven Poles of working age have worked abroad, be it seasonally, such as in helping with harvests in neighbouring countries, or more long-term. In 2014, between 1.8 and 2.1 million Polish men and women, mostly young people, were away from home, working abroad.

Coal is moved by a bucket wheel device in Łódź.

Sport in Poland

P oland is home to many sports stars, from top female tennis player Agnieszka Radwańska to leading ski jumper, Adam Małysz and four-time Olympic-gold-medal-winning racewalker, Robert Korzeniowski. Poland has also boasted world champions in a wide range of sports, from skiing and boxing to athletics and gymnastics.

NO WAY!

Polish weightlifter Waldemar Baszanowski set an incredible 24 world records during his career. He won two Olympic gold medals and was crowned world champion five different times.

Football Facts

Football is Poland's national sport, with over 400,000 men and women playing regularly. Top professional clubs include Legia Warsaw and Wisła Kraków, both of which have won the Polish national championships (held since 1921) more than 10 times. Many of Poland's leading players today, including goalkeeper Wojciech Szczęsny and striker Robert Lewandowski, play for foreign clubs but turn out for their national team. In 2012, Poland co-hosted the 2012 European Championships along with neighbours, Ukraine. Two years later, Poland beat world champions, Germany, in Warsaw for the very first time in front of over 56,900 fans.

 Robert Lewandowski shoots during Poland's match against Greece at Euro 2012.

Having a Ball

Other ball sports beside football attract lots of interest in Poland. Handball is played frequently, while basketball is popular both as a casual game for fun and as a spectator sport, with the top professional players competing in the 16-team DBE league. Volleyball is another popular sport, with the Men's Volleyball World Championship hosted in seven Polish cities during 2014. Poland triumphed over Brazil in the final to be crowned world champions.

The PlusLiga is the top level of competition for professional volleyball players in Poland.

Start Your Engines!

Polish speedway stars Adam Skornicki and Krzysztof Jablonski race hard at Poznań.

Motorsports are big in Poland, especially motorcycle speedway in which bikes with plenty of power but no brakes race round laps of an oval dirt track. At the top level of competition in Poland, the Ekstraliga, 10,000 or 15,000 spectators turn out to watch a race night. Polish riders are among the best in the world and Poland won the Speedway World Cup six times between 2006 and 2014. Poland's first Formula One driver, Robert Kubica, moved from track to rally racing and now competes in the World Rally Championship which includes the famous Rally of Poland. This was first held in 1923, making it the second oldest rally race in the world.

Great Gdańsk

Poland's biggest port, Gdańsk has an amazing history stretching back well over 1,000 years. A prosperous centre of trade, by the 1750s the city was the largest in eastern Europe. For almost 20 years of the 20th century (1920-39) it was even the centre of its own mini-nation, the Free City of Danzig, and was where the very first battle of World War II was fought, in September 1939, as German troops invaded.

Ships and Shipbuilding

Lying on the mouth of the Motława River where it empties into the Baltic Sea, Gdańsk grew into a major European port and Poland's centre of shipbuilding. It is connected by the Vistula River to Poland's capital, Warsaw, and is the country's largest port. In 2013, it handled over 30.2 million tonnes of cargo, mostly coal, oil, petroleum and more than a million standard containers carrying everything from foods to washing machines.

NO WAY!

Gdańsk's St Mary's Church (below) is thought to be the largest brick church in the world and has space inside to hold up to 25,000 people! That's roomy! There are 400 steps to climb to reach the top of its tower.

18

Solidarity

The Gdańsk shipyard saw the birth of an important political movement when workers started striking in 1980. They formed a trade union known as Solidarity led by a shipyard electrician, Lech Walesa. At its height, Solidarity boasted over 10 million members but was outlawed by the Polish government. Its members continued to campaign for workers' rights and in 1990 when free elections for the country were held, Lech Walesa was elected Poland's president.

The Solidarity sign became famous all around the world.

Local Landmarks

The Żuraw Crane could lift heavy loads 11m into the air and operated for 500 years.

Visitors to Gdańsk flock to the Main Town (the old quarter of the city) where beautiful, rebuilt or restored houses and galleries line quaint, narrow streets. Found along Długi Targ (Long Market) is the city's famous fountain of Neptune, first erected in 1549 but taken apart and hidden to save it from damage during World War II. Along the waterfront can be found the Żuraw Crane, which could lift loads of up to 2,000kg and was the biggest crane in medieval Europe.

Religion and Tradition

Compared to some nations in Europe, Poland remains a religious country. Around nine in ten of all its population are Roman Catholic and around half attend a church service at least once a week. Poland also has around half a million followers of the Eastern Orthodox Church and smaller numbers of Jews, Jehovah's Witnesses, Protestants and Muslims.

Churches Old and New

Poland is packed with places of worship including historic wooden churches like Haczów Church (built in 1388) and early brick churches including St Mary's Basilica in Kraków. One of Poland's newest Roman Catholic churches is also its biggest. The Basilica of Our Lady of Licheń was designed by the architect Barbara Bielecka. At 120m long, 77m wide and 141.5m high it is one of the largest in Europe, yet it is located in the village of Licheń Stary which is home to just 1,100 people.

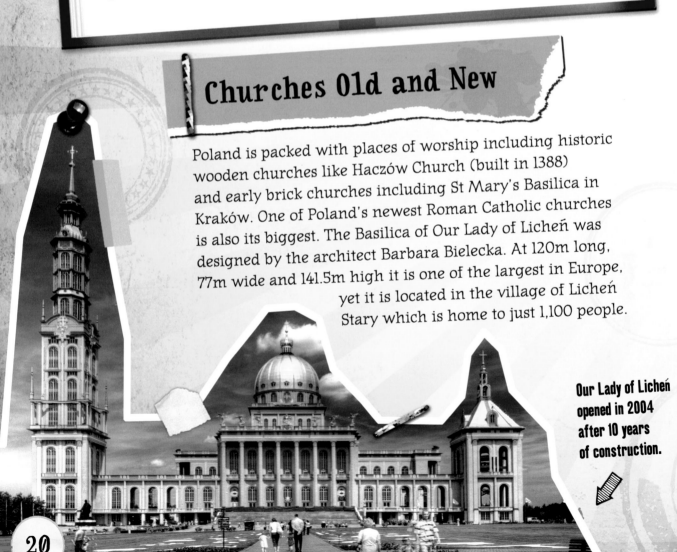

Our Lady of Licheń opened in 2004 after 10 years of construction.

A Polish Pope

Born in Wadowice, southern Poland, Karol Wojtyla studied languages at Jagiellonian University before training to become a priest during World War II. He became Archbishop of Kraków in 1964 and 14 years later was elected the first Pope (head of the Roman Catholic Church) not to be from Italy since 1523. As Pope John Paul II, the globetrotting religious leader visited 129 countries, covering 1.1 million km in the process. He remains a hero, after his death in 2005, to many Poles.

NO WAY!

As a young man, the future Pope John Paul II loved football, supported Polish team, Cracovia Cracow and played in matches at school and university as a goalkeeper.

This statue of Pope John Paul II is in his home town of Wadowice.

Upholding Traditions

Easter and Christmas, especially Christmas Eve, are major religious celebrations in Poland, while many Poles observe other traditions. These include Imieniny or name day – a day on which people with the same first name as a particular Polish saint, such as Irena and Wincenty on 5 April or Stefan and Maria on 15 August, celebrate with their family and friends. Many families weave straw dolls, called Marzanny, which represent winter. Children throw the dolls into a river during the month of March to represent the end of winter.

These people are taking part in a Good Friday Easter procession.

The Poles at Play

Polish people enjoy many of the same leisure pursuits as other Europeans, from watching one of the dozens of Polish TV channels to reading, surfing the web and socializing with friends. Come holiday time, most Poles travel inside their country's borders, visiting the northern coast, grappling with the great outdoors in the Masurian Lakes or Tatra Mountains or staying in historic cities such as Kraków or Warsaw. The increased availability of budget flights into Poland has meant that millions of foreign visitors can experience the same places as Poles.

Out in the Country

With a wide variety of countryside, it's no surprise that many Poles head for the hills...or lakes or plains in their spare time. Leisure pursuits such as kayaking, sailing, cycling and horse riding are all extremely popular. Many Poles like to go walking or climbing. Poland's Tatra Mountains provide skiing and winter sport opportunities and frozen lakes allow ice skating out in the open.

 Polish cowboys enjoy a three-day trek close to the Table Mountains.

Urban Treats

Around 61 per cent of all Poles live in towns and cities where they enjoy typical pursuits such as the cinema, music concerts and the theatre. Most urban areas have well-developed leisure and sports centres, which offer swimming, athletics, tennis, basketball and football among other sports. Most Poles are very family-orientated so spending leisure time with their families, having a coffee or cake out at a café or taking a walk around a city park are common pastimes.

The Grand Theatre and National Opera in Theatre Square, Warsaw.

Life's a Beach

As a northern European country better known for its snowy mountain ranges, many visitors are surprised by Poland's sunny beaches. Despite bordering the chilly Baltic Sea, Poland's 700km northern coastline contains many sandy beaches to which thousands of Poles flock in the summer. Temperatures can rise above 30ºC in July and August so visitors can enjoy sunbathing, swimming and watersports such as windsurfing. Sopot is a popular beach resort city that is home to the longest wooden pier in Europe, stretching out 512m into the sea.

A beach on Usedom, an island split between Germany and Poland.

NO WAY!

Ice boats glide over the slippery surface of the frozen Masurian lakes in winter. The fastest of these can race along far quicker than they could sail on water – as fast as 100km/h.

Art and Music

Poland has a long history of artistic endeavour in painting, sculpture, music and literature. Movies by famous film directors such as Krzysztof Kieslowski and Roman Polanski have been seen in cinemas all over the world. Visitors flock to art galleries too, sites such as Wroclaw, currently home to the gigantic 15m-high, 114m-long painting depicting a battle, known as the Racławice Panorama.

This statue of Chopin sitting under a willow tree is in Warsaw's Lazienki Park.

Home is Where The Heart is

Frederic Chopin is Poland's most famous musician and composer. He was born in Żelazowa Wola in 1810 and was giving public concerts by the age of eight. A prolific composer of classical piano pieces that are still played and enjoyed today, Chopin died in Paris at the age of 39. At his request, his body was buried in Paris but his heart was taken back to Poland where it is housed in an urn at Warsaw's Holy Cross Church.

You're Booked!

Among Poland's writers and poets are five Nobel Prize winners for Literature, the latest being poet Wisława Szymborska from Kraków. Poland's most famous author to foreigners is Józef Korzeniowsk. He is better known as Joseph Conrad, who left Poland for England where he wrote *Heart of Darkness*, *Nostromo* and *Lord Jim* – all of which have been turned into movies. Poland's leading science fiction author, Stanisław Lem, the writer of *Fiasco*, *His Master's Voice* and other novels, has also had his work turned into films, the most famous being *Solaris*. Lem has sold over 45 million copies of his books.

A monument in Gdynia to the writer Joseph Conrad (shown above right on a Polish stamp).

Folk Dancing and Modern Music

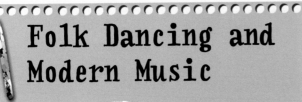

Polish folk dancing stems from many centuries ago. Many dances such as the Krakowiak and the Oberek are fast and acrobatic, involving jumps, twirls and quick stepping movements. They are often accompanied by musicians playing fiddles, mandolins, pipes, tambourines and a form of bagpipes called a kozioł. For those who like their music louder and more modern, there is a vibrant rock and metal scene in Poland, with bands such as Turbo, Desdemona, Hunter and Vader as well as hip-hop and rap acts including Liroy, Marysia Starosta and O.S.T.R.

The band Dzem performs to a crowd of fans in 2014.

Fabulous Festivals

M any holidays and festivals take place throughout the year in Poland. Some are religious, such as Easter and All Saints Day (November 1st) when families visit relatives' graves. Others, such as the Poznań Jazz Fair, the Short Film Festival in Kraków and the Borderlands Theatre Festival in Cieszyn, celebrate Poland's arts and culture.

Fireworks at Noc Kupaly

Fire and Flowers

An ancient festival is still held on the shortest night of the year (usually the 21st or 22nd of June). Called *Noc Kupały* or *Wianki*, the event is dedicated to fire and water. People light fires and then dance and sing around them or jump over them, as they believe the fire cleanses them and protects them against bad luck. In some places, people float candles or wreaths of flowers across a river. If they reach the other side, it is said the person will find love.

Fun Fests

During the Highland carnival at Bukowina Tatrzańska, people enjoy *kumoterki*, unusual skiing races in which skiers are towed by galloping horses. In other festivals people ride horses while dressed as armoured medieval knights, and during the Rękawka tournament in Kraków, held just after Easter, a full-blown re-enactment of a medieval battle takes place in celebration of the legendary founder of Kraków, Prince Krakus. For even more ancient fighting and fury, you could visit the Viking Festival, held every July in the Baltic coast town of Wolin.

Medieval soldiers advance during the Rekawka festival held at the foot of Krak's Mound in Kraków.

Wroclaw's guitarists raise their instruments into the air. Rock on!

Music Festivals

All sorts of music is celebrated and performed at a wide range of Polish music festivals. Every May in Wrocław, for example, thousands of budding guitarists flock to the city's market place. There, they all attempt to play the Jimi Hendrix song, *Hey Joe*. In 2014, a record 7,273 guitarists took part! The biggest music festival of all is Woodstock Poland, a huge free festival held in the open air near the Polish town of Kostrzyn nad Odrą. In 2014, the festival attracted close to 750,000 people!

Uniquely Polish

P oland is an unusual country. Few places have had to suffer invasion or fights for freedom over 40 times since 1600. Not many countries have a Gold Prospectors World Championship (held at Złotoryja every year), either. Here are some more unique attractions that make Poland a peculiarly special place to visit.

NO WAY!

During World War II, Polish soldiers adopted a Syrian brown bear which they named Wojtek. He was taught to salute, given the rank of private and even served in battle in Italy, carrying crates of ammunition. Wojtek survived the war and lived until 1963 in Edinburgh Zoo.

Salty Stuff

For over 800 years, people have mined salt in Wieliczka, around 10km from Kraków. The end result is nothing short of spectacular – and seriously strange. More than 300km of underground mine tunnels, the deepest more than 300m below ground, exist. These include caverns, underground lakes, dozens of statues and large underground chapels all made of rock salt. This astonishing site attracts more than a million visitors each year, many of whom post a postcard from the post office there, 125m underground.

The Chapel of St Kinga in the salt mines is located 101m below ground.

Bones Alone

If you're easily scared or creeped out, you might be best avoiding Kaplica Czaszek – a small chapel at Czermna. Built in 1776, the chapel's walls are decorated with around 3,000 human skulls and leg bones, all placed there by local priest Wacław Tomaszek over a period of 18 years. When he died in 1804, his skull joined the others in pride of place on the altar. What's more, there are the skeletal remains of a further 21,000 people buried below the chapel.

A creepy sight as leg bones form a latticework ceiling in part of the chapel.

Crooked House, Crooked Forest

The bowing windows and walls of the Crooked House.

Built in the city of Sopot in 2004, Krzywy Domek (meaning 'crooked little house') is an eye-poppingly bent and buckled house that is part of the Rezydent shopping centre. Its crazy design was inspired by fairy tale illustrations of Polish artists. There's more crookedness near the town of Gryfino in western Poland, where a strange woodland nicknamed the Crooked Forest can be found. It contains around 400 pine trees that have grown with a 90-degree bend in their trunk. Almost all of the trees are bending to point to the north.

The crazy Crooked Forest

29

More Information

Websites

http://www.polska.pl/en/experience-poland/traditions-and-holidays
Learn more about Polish traditions and key holidays at Poland's official website.

http://whc.unesco.org/en/statesparties/pl
View pictures and information on all 14 of Poland's UNESCO World Heritage sites.

http://bpn.com.pl/index.php?option=com_content&task=view&id=633&itemid=280&lang=en
Check out the European Bison and the other animals and plants found at the Bialowieski Park.

http://www.timeforkids.com/destination/poland/sightseeing
Click on this interactive map of Poland to view some of the country's most fascinating sites.

http://www.nationsonline.org/oneworld/poland.htm
A handy web page about Poland complete with map, facts and dozens of weblinks to websites about Polish history, culture and geography.

http://www.bbc.co.uk/news/world-europe-17754512
A useful timeline of Polish history from the BBC News website.

Apps

Poland.Travel
Packed with information provided by the National Polish Tourism Organisation.

My Warsaw
Interactive guide to Poland's capital city with walking routes and information on places of note.

Bhuio Talk Polish
Fun and helpful way to learn Polish words and phrases. Once downloaded, this app works offline, so you don't need an internet connection to use it.

Armaxis Chopin Complete Works
See the composer Frederic Chopin's sheet music and listen to it being played with this interesting app.

Clips

http://whc.unesco.org/en/list/32/video
Watch a video about the amazing Wieliczka salt mines brought to you by UNESCO.

https://www.youtube.com/watch?v=stEuQamTLXw
This is an animation about Poland's past and the battles fought during the country's history.

http://www.biography.com/people/marie-curie-9263538/videos/marie-curie-mini-biography-35738691933
Watch this clip about the life and achievements of pioneering Polish scientist, Marie Curie.

https://www.youtube.com/watch?v=V1Ph86alga8
Enjoy this short clip about ice boat racing across Poland's frozen lakes.

Books

Discover Countries: Poland
by Rosie Wilson (Wayland, 2013)

Poland by Heather Docalavich
& Shaina Indovino (Mason Crest, 2013)

The Ancient World: Ancient Maya
by Charlotte Guillain (Raintree, 2011)

Scientists Who Made History: Marie Curie
by Liz Gogerly (Wayland, 2014)

The Silver Sword by Ian Serraillier
(Vintage Children's Classics, 2012)

The national bird of Poland, the white-tailed eagle, is found on the country's coat of arms, wearing a gold crown.

Glossary

comet A body of dust and ice that orbits the Sun.

coniferous Describes trees that have needles or scaled leaves that tend to be evergreen and do not shed their leaves in autumn.

elected To be selected for a role or job by a vote of people.

European Union A union of many countries in Europe most of whom share a single currency, the Euro, and follow a number of shared laws and regulations.

lard A type of fat made from pigs which is used in cooking.

observatory A place from which astronomers can examine the night sky.

parliament A body that makes the laws of a country.

professional To be paid to do a job, such as to play a sport.

prosperous Having success or becoming wealthy.

rye A cereal crop, mostly grown in temperate or cool climates, the grain from which can be made into flour.

trade union An organization made up of workers from the same or similar industries formed to campaign and negotiate for an increase in pay or better working conditions.

tributary A stream or small river that flows into another, usually larger, waterway.

Index

Unpacked

Australia

Australia: Unpacked
Exploration and Discovery
City Sights
Not All Desert
Aussie Animals
Long Distance Travellers
Go, Aussie, Go!
Mine Time
On the Coast
Native Australians
Aussie Tucker
Everyday Life
Coming to Australia

978 0 7502 8424 0

Brazil

Brazil: Unpacked
A World of Faces
Let's Go to Rio!
Viva Futebol!
Jungle Giant
Nature's Treasure Trove
Highways and Skyways
Bright Lights, Big Cities
Life, Brazilian Style
Looking Good
Arts for All
Adventurous Tastes
Prepare to Party!

978 0 7502 8402 8

China

China: Unpacked
The Story of China
One in a Billion
Futuristic Cities
A World in One
Country Life
Going Places
Ancient Arts
Made in China
Be a Sport
Land of the Panda
Believe it!
Let's Eat Together

978 0 7502 9172 9

Croatia

Croatia: Unpacked
Kaleidoscope Country
Pay a Visit
Sea and Snow
Time-Travel Cities
Country Quiet
Playing Ball
In the Wild
Being Croatian
A Place in Europe
All You Can Eat
Festival Fun
Creative Croatia

978 0 7502 9163 7

Denmark

Denmark: Unpacked
Lowlands and Islands
Kings, Vikings and Castles
Royalty and Rulers
Colourful Copenhagen
Danish Delights
Danish Territories
A Sporting Nation
Trade and Power
Design for Life
That's Entertainment
Great Danes
A Happy People

978 0 7502 9160 6

France

France: Unpacked
The City of Light
Ruling France
Fruit of the Earth
Home and Away
Power and Progress
Grand Designs
Bon Appetit
The Arts
En Vacance
Made in France
Allez Sport
Life in France

978 0 7502 8416 5

Germany

Germany: Unpacked
Forests, Rivers and Lakes
East and West
Dinner Time!
Energy and Ecology
Knights and Castles
Football Crazy!
Super Cities
Big Brains
Great Days Out
The Car's the Star
Quirky Germany
All the Arts

978 0 7502 9166 8

India

India: Unpacked
From 0 to a Billion
Touring India
Everyone's Game
Wild Wonders
Rocks, Rivers, Rains
Life on the Land
High-tech, Low-tech!
Staggering Cities
Everyday India
Spice is Nice
Bollywood Beats
Bright Arts

978 0 7502 8417 2

Italy

Italy: Unpacked
The Romans
Rome: the Eternal City
Way to Go
Food Glorious Food
La Bella Figura
Mountains and Volcanoes
The Italian Arts
Calcio!
North and South
Everyday Life
Super Cities
Italian Inventions

978 0 7502 8401 1

Mexico

Mexico: Unpacked
Viva Mexico!
Land of Extremes
City Living
Wonders of the World
Working the Land
It's a Winner
On the Move
Going Wild
Lively Life
On the Money
Ready to Eat?
Amazing Arts

978 0 7502 9169 9

Poland

Poland: Unpacked
Wondrous Warsaw
The Land
Super Scientists
Food for Thought
Work and School
Sport in Poland
Great Gdańsk
Religion and Tradition
The Poles at Play
Art and Music
Fabulous Festivals
Uniquely Polish

978 0 7502 9157 6

Portugal

Portugal: Unpacked
Small Country, Big Story
Let's Play!
Holiday Hotspot
Sun, Sand and Serras
Island Magic
Charismatic Cities
Made in Portugal!
Country Corkers
Wild Times
Make Yourself at Home
Surf 'n Turf
Creative Culture

978 0 7502 8843 9

South Africa

South Africa: Unpacked
Three Capitals
The Land
Becoming South Africa
SA Sport
Farming
Rainbow Nation
Fabulous Food
Rich and Poor
Wild Life
Mineral Wealth
On the Coast
Holidays and Festivals

978 0 7502 8844 6

Spain

Spain: Unpacked
A World of Their Own
Fiesta Forever
On the Ball
Highlands and Islands
Sleepless Cities
Escape to the Country
Wild Spain
Spanish Life
All You Can Eat
Hola World!
Olé, Olé!
Eye-Popping Arts

978 0 7502 8425 7

WAYLAND
www.waylandbooks.co.uk